FLOATING CITY

FLOATING CITY

Poems

ANNE PIERSON WIESE

LOUISIANA STATE UNIVERSITY PRESS ⚜ BATON ROUGE

For Ben

Published by Louisiana State University Press
Copyright © 2007 by Anne Pierson Wiese
All rights reserved
Manufactured in the United States of America
An LSU Press Paperback Original
FIRST PRINTING

DESIGNER: Melanie O'Quinn Samaha
TYPEFACE: Adobe Garamond Pro
PRINTER AND BINDER: Edwards Brothers, Inc.

LIBRARY OF CONGRESS CATALOGING-IN-PUBLICATION DATA

Wiese, Anne Pierson.
  Floating city : poems / Anne Pierson Wiese.
    p. cm.
  ISBN-13: 978-0-8071-3235-7 (pbk. : alk. paper)
  I. Title.
PS3623.I385F66 2007
811'.6—dc22

                                        2006027370

Thanks to the editors of the following publications, in which these poems first appeared: *Alaska Quarterly Review,* "Needle and Thread" (2003); *Atlanta Review,* "The Distance" (2006); *Blue Mesa,* "On Learning to Go Limp in Public Places" (2003); *Borderlands: Texas Poetry Review,* "Airborne" (2004); *Carolina Quarterly,* "Inside" (2002); *Diner,* "Composed upon Brooklyn Bridge, July 6, 2003" (2004); *Hawai'i Pacific Review,* "Sugar Hill, Harlem" (2003), "in the garden at the time of the evening breeze" (2006); *The Ledge,* "Death Has No Place" (2000); *The Nation,* "The Century Plant" (2004); *Porcupine,* "You Are Here" (2001), "Hermit Coming Out of the Forest" (2006), "Wind Farm" (2006); *Prairie Schooner,* "In the Garden" (2003), "Mica Schist" (2006); *Quarterly West,* "Casa Rosa," "Silver Palace," "Last Night in Brooklyn," "Water Bug," "Tante Ethel in the Willow" (all 2003); *Raritan,* "A Pole, a Fence, a Bridge" (2006); *Rattapallax,* "Season's Greetings from South Dakota" (2002); *Saint Ann's Review,* "Leaving Brooklyn Heights" (2002), "Everything but God" (2004); *South Carolina Quarterly,* "Undergrowth" (2003), "Gift Basket for a Madman" (2006); *West Branch,* "Columbus Park" (2003), "Farmers" (2003), "The Great Roberto" (2005), "How We Memorize" (2005).

  "In the Beginning" first appeared in *The Arvon International Poetry Competition Anthology, 2004: He Drew Down Blue from the Sky to Make a River,* ed. Jamie McKendrick (London: Arvon Foundation, 2004). "Profile of the Night Heron" first appeared in *The "Discovery"/The Nation 30th Anniversary Program @ 92nd St. Y* (2004).

CONTENTS

One IN THE GARDEN

Two LAST NIGHT IN BROOKLYN

Three WIND FARM

One

IN THE GARDEN

Profile of the Night Heron ✓

In the Brooklyn Botanic Garden the night
heron is on his branch of his tree, blue
moon curve of his body riding low
above the pond, leaves dipping into water
beneath him, green and loose as fingers.
On the far shore, the ibis is where
I left him last time, a black cypher
on his rock. These birds, they go to the right
place every day until they die.

There are people like that in the city,
with signature hats or empty attaché cases,
expressions of private absorption fending
off comment, who attach to physical
locations—a storefront, a stoop, a corner,
a bench—and appear there daily as if for a job.
They negotiate themselves into the pattern
of place, perhaps wiping windows, badly,
for a few bucks, clearing the stoop of take-out
menus every morning, collecting the trash
at the base of the WALK/DON'T WALK sign
and depositing it in the garbage can.

Even when surfaces change, when the Mom & Pop
store becomes a coffee bar, when the park
benches are replaced with dainty chairs and a pebble
border, they stay, noticing what will never change:
the heartprick of longitude and latitude
to home in on, the conviction that life
depends, every day, on what outlasts you.

The Century Plant

The century plant's flowered spear appears
only once, twenty feet tall, shortly before
its death. Given the proper conditions, all plants
bloom on schedule. We are less sure
of ourselves, the conditions we make
for presenting what's inside us
to the world less specific; we are haunted
by unplantlike doubts about the worth
of what we have to offer. The Botanic
Garden had advertised the event. I don't
remember how old I was, maybe ten.
There was a once-in-a-lifetime line
in the conservatory, a familiar smell
of growth and decay, the choice to look or look away.

Mica Schist

St. Nicholas Park in Harlem is one of few spots
on the island of Manhattan where you can stand
on terraces of rock untouched since men
with surveyor's tools stood on them
to deliver the bad news, back in the last
century but one: Gentlemen, here is a substance
we cannot move. So they built around,
below and above, leaving this uneven
pleat of ground, rocks surfaced between the trees
like whales in strips of sun, stunned to find themselves
landlocked among buildings, illuminated
at night by lamp posts. The old maples and oaks,
roots plumbing the hill as humans could not,
whisper of what's below: more rock—more rock—more rock.

All Night Long

The first warm evening in spring—the evening
on which you no longer feel the air's
temperature and are only aware
of it as an invisibility draped
with sounds: laughter from open windows,
the idle of cars pausing at the curb,
abdominal wails presaging a cat
fight in some dark, disputed corner; draped
with smells: through a side door propped ajar fish
hitting hot oil, dust or mold from the pit
of a deserted construction site, the soil
in front gardens after rain, released
and crumbled from beneath by the numberless
green thumbs of spring's long reach up

out of the ground. A young man waits on the stoop
of a six-floor walkup with the posture
of someone who expects to wait
for a long time. What you imagine to be
his earthly possessions are beside him
in a shopping cart, along with a roll
of rubber foam, neatly tied. You imagine
he has come knowing there will be no bed,
only floor space in one of the apartments
above. You can't imagine more than this, so you
walk up the fading street to where the first
crocuses are out, each one a small, violet-shuttered
hesitation imbued with its own brevity,
knowing neither happiness nor grief.

Lilacs

Today the snow is melting in the streets, lunar
gray lumps riddled with dogs' piss and the pulp
of several weeks' worth of trash—disintegrated
newspapers, take-out food containers pecked apart
by pigeons, losing lotto tickets, here and there a trampled
glove, its five fingers splayed beneath the dingy ice
like the farewell wave of a dying civilization.

We forget—or never knew—how many of us have come
and gone, and for how long, but spring is on its way again
making everything green and clean and new. . . .
Even in the city, sloshing through the noxious
leavings of our winter's waste, we lift our faces
to the blue sky, catch the scent of lilacs blowing
in from somewhere—blowing, blowing one more time.

Undergrowth

When you were a kid you pretended
to be blind—closed your eyes, held a stick
out in front, suddenly weightless, thick
as invisible air, unable to step

where moments before there was no wall.
Now the wall at the edge of the world stinks
of dead leaves, dog feces, sounds like cold links
of swing sets in the park where fall

was bright collage bits until you felt
compelled to be blind. Now you're stuck
out on the limb of intention, telling
yourself to move forward while the suck
of breath in your chest unearths your heart lightly
as a stone raised by the roots of a tree.

In the Garden

On the edge of the pond a great white
egret catches five-inch fish, its trick neck
now a bone-china handle just thick
enough to curve without cracking—sleight

of spine and cup—now a javelin in flight
traveling with frugal grace: quickness
made slow by the instinct that missing
what's aimed for's what comes of haste, or *eyes*

too big for your stomach. Among the weeds' dead
shoots giant carp feed—a tea party of stiff-
tongued brutes sipping algaed shadows, exempt
by size from a predator whose slight kisses
yield up what's small enough to swallow instead
of choking alone on a single wish.

Sonnet to Basil

The seeds in the packet were so tiny and dry,
all fallen into the bottom fold like blue grit—
it was hard to believe that even one would sprout—
so I planted them all in the window box. Why

not? What was there to lose? Soon, a multitude
of minute green heads emerged from the damp soil,
pushing every day toward the light, toiling
with what came to seem heartbreaking certitude,

since every day, for the good of those final four
plants that would need room to fully mature,
I plucked the living threads out like a grim reaper
in training, each uprooting feeling more

brutal than the last, each frail sprout between
my finger and thumb a dumb reproach.

Ficus *Noire*

Almost eight years ago, in southern California,
I bought a ficus seedling in a supermarket.
The sale of potted plants in supermarkets
was a novelty to me. This specific ficus
looked small and lonely. So was I. Six inches
high at most, its several slender green stems
already bore a few of the signature
ficus leaves people love—deep green, glossy, and fish
shaped, each one hung individually,
together creating the impression
of movement—a school of minnows or green cloud
of butterflies. But this one wasn't there, yet.
Its size allowed it to be no more than a hint
of tree, which was fine by me, especially
since I needed to take it home
on an airplane to New York City. It rode
easily in the overhead compartment,
and made the strange journey safely.

Since then it's lived in three or four apartments
and several different pots, each one larger
than the last. I always position it by the best
window and water it only once
a week—but thoroughly—to promote deep root
growth. By now it's bigger than I am; its stems
have hardened into a grove of trunks. It won't fit
in the shower anymore, much less go out the front
door, so it looks like I'm here to stay. Acquaintances
say it's taking over—and laugh. But little
do they know I am dreaming of the day
I will walk into the forest.

Spring Planting

I

First we clear the winter refuse from the ground
around the tree. It's mostly small stuff: bottle
caps, bleached cigarette butts, the odd metro
card, partial plastic wraps off unknown objects,
a shattered crack pipe glinting like ice from beneath
ivy. We are delicate, as if by noticing
each item we can forgive its presence.
My husband says he's found half a counterfeit
dime. I find this hard to believe—who'd bother
counterfeiting dimes? He shows it to me,
a jagged metal crescent, its markings erased
by weather. He slips it into his pocket
when he thinks I'm not looking. Later, I'll find
it at the bottom of the washing machine.

II

Growing flowers in the city is not easy.
Every sidewalk passerby represents
potential hazard. All dogs urinate. Certain people
defoliate. Others like the plants so much
they want them for their own; some mornings
we find small holes crumbling in on themselves
at the edges of the bed, as though someone thought
we might not notice if he or she took them
strategically. It's hard to grudge a flower.
Balls bounce the wrong way, bottles get thrown.
Once, on big trash day, the garbage men lost
their grip on a paisley love seat clawed
to ribbons by a cat. Luckily, it was early
in the season and we were able to replant.

III

It's taxing work for us middle-aged, bookish
types. We stand by our plot in the cool
morning air, noting the faint haze in the sky
over the river, knowing that tomorrow
we will wake sore, pull on our clothes, and race
downstairs to see whether the plants made it through
their first night. Our side of the street gets the afternoon
light, so impatiens do well, petunias lift
their bright trumpets, pink and white, beside thick-lipped
begonias. Now, if we get the right amounts of rain
and sun, they will cease looking like so many lives
placed willy-nilly where no life should be, and begin
to take hold, grasping the ground with invisible hands,
unfurling up, undaunted, into the surrounding world.

Peony

I notice myself growing older most
among other growing things: the green
progression in the garden from furled, tacky
shoots still showing red, to blue hands shingling
the air with lush, deceptive authority,
to the end of summer when even
a dilatory breeze lightens the trees
of another hundred or so gaunt-stemmed leaves.

The fullness of the peony's magenta bloom
billowing around its heart of saffron shreds rings
in my chest like noon. And the faint way the flower
starts to age, with only an initial ripple
of its outer skin, strikes me like a forgotten
task—something I only half meant to do.

Hermit Coming Out of the Forest

How hard it is on the ears, the first
shattering of human voices. Even far
away, they are too loud, they crowd the air.
The birds, who are in the habit of listening
to each other and measuring
the significance of silence
between calls, are wholly silent here; no bugs'
chorus times its harsh rattle; the coal blue wasp
on his mathematical rounds does not come here;
nor can I hear the frog's murky pause.
Each year, at forest's edge, I have to promise myself
never again, leave the fullness of my senses
like a brown cloak pooled in the brush, go forward
on bare feet, nerve bared, skeletal as hope.

Rabid

At first I thought the squirrel was caught
in the fence, screaming, dangling by one paw.
But then I saw that it was holding on
as it convulsed—like an animal electrified
in a cartoon. It was so inexplicable
that I stood watching and wondering
at the edge of the park, to which I'd walked
hoping to see the red and orange fall leaves
I remembered from the year before. However,
all the trees seemed to be yellow and brown
this time around, and the squirrel kept twisting
and screaming, its white belly exposed and gleaming.
Finally, it dropped to the sidewalk where I
expected it would lie still. But it did not.

It kept convulsing, flipping itself
frantically in the dust and litter
at the base of the fence, emitting squeal
after enraged squeal, until at last it seemed
to regain a measure of control, flattening
itself on the ground as if the ground
were a tree, and advancing across the pavement
in my direction with the fitful motion
and chatter of an insect. The enriched autumn
light flashed retractor-like into the sidewalk's
crannies and flaws. It lit the dying daisies
at the park's rim with a cold beam, penetrated
the evergreen bushes to their trunks. I pulled
my coat closer around me and crossed the street.

How much in life comes to some kind of internal
burning, ordinary existence occurring
in the spaces before or after—the leaf's

span of green, the walk in the park, the dream
of many days—nudged on either side by birth and grief.

Meanwhile, the squirrel had crawled into the street
where it was squashed mid-squeak by the left front
tire of a red livery cab barreling
on its way without pause. For a long time
I stayed, watching the small body, which never
moved until another car passed over it
and set its tail—still intact—fluttering in the faint
blue exhaust. The falling white light settled
level with the parking meters—then died.

in the garden at the time of the evening breeze
(Genesis 3:8)

Showers on and off all day, light drained of edges.
Along the pavement, umbrellas flat
as flowers on garden flagstones after rain.
Skyscrapers rooted wet and vegetable,
making vague green cathedrals
of the streets. People's faces turned to the harbor
wind's honey sting of sleep—eight million
dreams of paradise persist, migrant mist
on the mirror of this metal made flesh.

On these days, we are a city floating
lonely as a water lily,
lapped by elements, rich in isolation
from our race, no tongue too foreign to bloom,
no lordly hand to tear us from our stem.

Two

LAST NIGHT IN BROOKLYN

In the Beginning

There was the famous photographer, Walker Evans,
who started by photographing old signs and ended
by filling his bathtub with them and washing
himself in the kitchen sink. There was the Harlem
man whose pet tiger cub grew so big that first
his family and finally he himself fled
the 12th-floor, three-bedroom apartment in the housing
project, returning every day to fling raw chickens
through a crack in the front door. Love displaces

everything. All over the city the signs peer
from beneath modern façades, fade in the sun and rain
high up on sides of buildings: BEST QUALITY TWINE. Ghosts
on brick, cockeyed atop demolition dumpsters, tin
worn delicate as paper, pale lettered—mint,
red, black: ELEVATOR APARTMENTS AVAILABLE:
INQUIRE ON PREMISES. If you stare at them words
are faces; everyone who ever spelled them out,
ever debated whether to buy twine or rent
an apartment fades up into view wearing shadowy
Homburgs, black veils, parcels in their arms, the winter
air freshening for snow. Or imagine the face
of a tiger waiting behind a thin metal door,
your furniture demolished, your family living
on friends' floors, your neighbors smelling urine and fur
and losing their tolerance, a policeman
rappelling outside your windows with a dart gun.

Imagine a hunger for the invisible world
so deep it must have existed before you were born.

The Taking

In the morning on my way to the subway
I pass disemboweled trash bags
at the curb, in front of the big building
down the block. You can tell how people dug things out
overnight by street light, or in the drizzle-lit dawn,
carrying some away, but others only a certain
distance—maybe ten steps, maybe fifty yards—before
deciding upon inspection that after all they
were not worth the taking. A child's stained pink sweatshirt hung
neatly on a fence, a rusty saucepan like a hat
on a hydrant, a bundle of old magazines
rippled by the damp on the hood of a parked car—
each item taken carefully and as carefully
dismissed, for reasons known only to those who disappear.

Casa Rosa

Casa Rosa in the old days, before
it got sold, was manned by a woman who sat
at the end of the bar balancing her fat
platinum do. *Hello, Sweetheart. Table for*

two. Smug as a white toad in a pantsuit. *The Lord
knows I try.* On the red wall the Pope and
the painting of a girl in an appliqué hat
from 1945. The mystery wore

well among the antique rifles hung
cocked near the ceiling of stamped tin.
Now the ceiling's been sheetrocked, revolution
no longer sleeps in the subterranean
Fra Diavolo orders of older men who hummed
"Volare" with the anisette, Rosa's evening hymn.

Silver Palace

In Chinatown they wash the tables with tea
as pale as night water—spilled
with a single dip of the wrist, still
steaming, from its metal pot—gleefully

affronting tourists who sit uneasily
at a round communal table half willing
but unable to let the space filling
their wide laps go. The tea spreads, a busy sea

eking toward the table's edge. Some waiters
wait until chairs are scraped back to soak
it up with a napkin or two. Later,
in the kitchen, a cook just woken
up from a nap considers dizzy Fate
who keeps putting together people like hope.

Last Night in Brooklyn

There is a sheen of traffic noise
on the expressway—not a sound so much
as the absence of sleep. Dutch
settlers with their staffs, Van Brunt and Van Nuyse,

ended journeys and began, pancake blue hats poised
to slip from their heads into the wan dust
of coast roads like maps, followed their wanderlust
here, tracks of salt, cheese rinds tossed to porpoises

in the bay, arriving fires in the damp
night, scrounging the ground for good flat rocks,
leaving metal, bones, broken bits, fine china, hoists
of rope cached deep below these cement ramps'
unpresent hum. 3 A.M. The digital clock
glows. Out my window clings the moon—mum as an oyster.

Sugar Hill, Harlem

Across Convent Avenue, five floors up
a woman hangs her clean laundry to dry
out three adjacent windows—one piece
at a time. I glimpse her green turban
sailing from room to room like a tropical bird
determined to locate a palm tree—
method is everything when you try
for the impossible. All night her lights' abrupt
mirage wavers from behind garments that
give way, one soft-limbed shape to the next,
absorbing this high washed air, white petaled
dark, water breeze pooling against silent metal
casements that look straight onto our lives—hexed
by journeys, charmed back by the tasks we work at.

Where We Live

Like many prewar apartment buildings, this one
has a name: Convent Court after its location
on Convent Avenue in New York. Built in a time
of luxury now gone, its grand details—the good stone,
the traces of terra-cotta, the time-dimmed
marble, the generous proportions—are still
stubbornly apparent beneath the signs
of neglect—sections of cornice razed rather
than repaired, lintels like sagging eyelids over
windows wide open in cold weather to combat
ancient radiators with broken shutoff valves.
Word on the block is that many of the apartments
have been illegally subdivided and sublet
to recent immigrants from Africa.

In winter, the young men walk through the snow
with bare ankles beneath the ornate hems
of their robes, fabrics bright as jewels half-swathed
by drab jackets too thin to be warm.
We native New Yorkers, trammeled with boots
and parkas, watch bemused as they stride
through freezing mornings with legs made of fire.

In the basement of the building an impromptu mosque
has sprung up, accessible down a flight of stairs
from the street, the musical call to prayer rising faint
and foreign onto the avenue as the men—many
of them street vendors or cab drivers—appear from all
directions, invisible in the city as they carry
on with living, but visible—no, luminous—
                              in the beeline toward belief.

Death Has No Place

Perhaps the fact of death would seem less strange
if out my bedroom window and below
there were a family graveyard in the snow
where those like me who have gone before change
only by familiar yards the arrangement
of their sleep; if my own place I could know
below such white, specific, well-known snow,
perhaps my death would seem a mere exchange.

But here in the city death has no place—
like drifting smoke it's exiled to the air,
long aloft before it breaks into space,
tossed with rain and exhaust, thin as despair;
here, since death appears and leaves us no trace,
I'm afraid to go without knowing where.

Airborne √

This morning I woke to helicopters and church
bells. From my window I watched the heavy blue
police birds circle over and back, over and back
against the gray sky which moved in unobtrusive
opposition—whatever happens below,
what blood-handed humans hide, it's a matter
of inconsequence to the large, cloaked order
of clouds untouchably processing—while inside
our building Deacon Holness emerged
from the apartment next to mine in his suit
and tie, thick eyeglasses tinted against the light
of evil, padded shoulders lifting across our street
toward the church, as if belief could make a man a cloud.

At the Laundromat

It's a large Laundromat with a glass front.
In the summer they keep the street doors
wide open and you can hear people
arguing on the pay phones outside,
or congregating in front of the grocery
store we call Rotten Foodtown. Not a lot
of air-conditioning around here. The sparrow
must have strayed in through the open doors. I
didn't notice it until it hit
the plate glass behind my seat, trying
to fly out, and rebounded stunned at my feet,
a soft heap of feathers with winking, alarmed
eyes. Hard to tell if it was injured or only
shocked. No more shocked than I—my heart took
on the lightness of the bird. What to do—

what to do? This sudden collision
of wings with human things made me want
to turn away, as if from unseemliness.

However, my duty was clear. A vague
memory of having been told never to touch
a bird with bare hands made me beg a rag
from the phlegmatic Laundromat attendant. As I
enclosed it, the sparrow fluttered slightly
and then was still while I carried it—ran
with it—to a triangle of greenery
at a nearby intersection of streets, reminding
myself my role was only courier between worlds,
my hope only good one bird at a time.

At the Farmer's Market

I rummage through a box of Kirbys, picking
out the smallest ones to make pickles. The dust
is still on them, their collective smell rising
slight and sweet as I tumble them back and forth
like a stone-polishing machine on the boardwalk.

I remember two weeks ago, our last night
in Paris: my husband, speaking no French
but managing to express such enthusiasm
for the *haricots verts* the woman behind the wine
bar has brought out in a carton from the kitchen
to snap in between customers, that she shrugs
and plops down a handful in front of us
on the wooden bar, gesturing to him—*let's
see what you can do.* After a few minutes
she says to me, "Il est vite," and pours
us each another glass of grand reserve madiran,
the gesture making us giddier than the wine.

When I bring my overloaded sack up to weigh,
the young South American worker wants
to know what I will do with nine pounds
of cucumbers. "Pickles," I say. He jokes, "Please,
bring some here." In the spring, he tells me, he bought seeds
to grow the dill blossoms you need to make pickles
but cannot buy in any store, and then had no
time to plant them. "It's strange. I work on a farm.
But I had no time . . ." "Yes," I reply, "It's ironic."
He looks pleased. "Ironic, yes. I knew what
it meant, but not how to pronounce it." As I
pay him, and he searches the deep pockets
of his canvas apron for change, I imagine
him repeating the story to another
customer, testing the word—shining it.

The Great Roberto

Cooking bare chested to avoid staining
his good shirt, he stirs the risotto,
pours champagne into crystal flutes, sews
black bass into parchment painstakingly.

What we want to know is: *Where's your bed?*
The apartment is 300 square feet
and we can't locate it. *No—really,*
where is it? He waves at the long banquet

table and the cocktail bar he's improvised
with a board and French linen: *Relax.*
Do you know the trick to risotto? He extracts
a one-ounce orange box, passes it before our eyes:

Truffle powder. A pinch. His long fingers
linger wand-like above the pot—then flicker.

The Weather in New York

The first flakes of a winter storm float
casually out of a low white sky. Along
with many other office workers I am
in line at a deli waiting to buy lunch.

People glance out the front window,
nod ominously at one another.

Bits of conversation sift through
the lines—the sandwich line, the hot
food line, the self-serve coffee line: we've seen
this all before, we've never seen this before.

When it's my turn to order, the young
man making sandwiches asks me if I
like this weather. I tell him that having
grown up here, I am used to it, which amounts
to the same thing. He tells me that in Morocco
the days are warm, the nights chilly and damp.
He touches the stainless-steel counter
with one fingertip. *There, when you come outside
in the early morning, you touch the cars
and they are wet. If you buy a new car
or a new bicycle, in one year it is all
rust.* I would like to ask him more
about Morocco, but mindful
of the people behind me, I do not.

Waiting in line to pay, I clutch my paper bag
on which he has scribbled an indecipherable
price and stare out at the snow—falling more
urgently now, as if for the first or last time.

Thanksgiving ✓

Somewhere downtown there is a parade flocked by crowds
of adults in parkas carrying take-out coffee
and ministering to their children. *Let the kids
in front* is a phrase being repeated up and down
Broadway. Up and down Broadway the kids, in front,
are looking back through the crowd every thirty seconds
to make sure their parents haven't disappeared,
their experience of the clowns and floats and bands
becoming fractured and anxious. For many,
these events are more fun in retrospect.

Uptown, I am watching the weather. A cold
front bearing high winds, dark clouds, and bursts
of blue is coming through, the air so brittle
that the soft rain shatters against it into pins.

Nevertheless, there is the sound of heavy rain:
fallen leaves driven down the middle
of the empty street, their scrape and sweep
indistinguishable from the smack of water
hitting rock. With each gust of wind, from the tree
outside my window more brown leaves fly up
like startled birds, descending in lengthy spirals
to lodge damply on the windshields of parked cars
and at the curb. Close by, someone is practicing
the trumpet, holding each note until
it dwindles out from under the diaphragm.

At street level, our neighbor is leaving the building
with his two young children. They are all carrying
shopping bags, going to the car, going away.

I may imagine myself to be a monk
at the window of my cell in the monastery,

choosing to record life with various additions
of detail—here a shadow in gold leaf,
there a small blue beast, on the facing page
a rose bush with prominent thorns—looking up
occasionally to measure how much light
is left in the sky because candles are hard
to come by, and finally pushing aside frail
regret along with my colors to join the others
for the evening, but even so it all comes back
to children marching into life armed with a bright
uncertainty that promises, at whatever cost,
to renew itself. *Let the kids in front so they can see.*

Leaving Brooklyn Heights

This gray March a shimmer runs gas blue
from the service station, elliptic pink
and green across the surface of the rain. Think
of numbered hopscotch squares drawn askew

with colored chalk—here the sidewalk newly
pebble paved, there hundred-fifty-year-old slates hitched
up by horses from the river—history
blank as time when you don't measure it. Two

surfaces made separate sounds beneath
my roller skates, one rough, one smooth
to ply the chalk along; thirty years later brief
in my mind's ear, the streaming horses soothed
Easy! as stone obliterated mud—all griefs
lost and washed in the gleaming cataract of youth.

Columbus Park

Down at the end of Baxter Street, where Five Points
slum used to be, just north of Tombs, is a pocket park.
On these summer days the green plane trees' leaves
linger heavy as a noon mist above
the men playing mah jongg—more Chinese
in the air than English. The city's composed
of village greens; we rely on the Thai
place on the corner: Tom Kha for a cold,
jasmine tea for fever, squid for love, Duck Yum
for loneliness. Outside, the grove of heat,
narrow streets where people wrestle rash and unseen
angels; inside, the coolness of a glen and the wait staff
in their pale blue collars offering ice water.
Whatever you've done or undone, there's a dish for you
to take out or eat in: spice for courage, sweet for chagrin.

Early Bird

After a swim at the Riverbank State
Park indoor pool, I walk back along
the ice-tracked path. The acres of grass
are still green beneath the snow.
I know my body, the way you do
after exercise—each reach of muscle and stop
of bone. *Morning to you.* Clinging to the orange
fence, with a view of the white and empty
track, is an old man, stout black shoes resting
on the bottom rung, gloveless hands clutching
the top. *I'm doing my exercise, too. I used
to keep three parakeets, see, and this is what
they did: climbed up the side of their cage and held
tight. See? It's easy—you just hang on and breathe.*

Gift Basket for a Madman

I

People boarding the subway car react
one of two ways: most ignore him, sitting
or standing in his vicinity
not with indifference, but without
curiosity. Warily, others exit
the car. His caravan of supermarket
cart and deluxe baby stroller is secured
to a pole by a series of expert knots
against the movement of the train,
while behind it he sleeps, ensconced
across three seats, enormous, barbarically
bearded, wrapped in coats, snoring with the gusto
that precedes waking. The intimacy
is inescapable, yet we escape it.

II

His possessions are a puzzle cube
of parts: broken boxes bleeding Easter
grass and newsprint, stray springs, half a piece of powder
blue luggage, marred hinges hung with splintered Christmas
balls, bicycle handles wired to the rack
of a much-used broiler pan, detached antennas
and rubber tubing, pinwheels, a child's missile toy,
chopsticks and plastic knives, toothbrushes, shocks
of immortelles culled from some luncheon bouquet,
and, atop it all, a jaunty array of fast food cups
with red, white, and blue straws, shadow liquid
braking with the train. On the cart's rear bumper,
affixed with electrician's tape—dog-eared escutcheon
of the soul—a hardware store sign reads: NOT FOR SALE.

Evening Rush

There is the tremble in the throat
of the tunnel before you hear it, movement
deep as a groin in the ground, a passion
of motion described by the MTA
as mass transit, but recognized by lovers
of subways as transportation
of another kind. Under the streets
we flock together, fleet and half tame
as rare birds loose in a cavernous
pet emporium, returning for the night
to their rows of pagodas. There is a sift
of wings against metal, electric
curtain of doors, departure's warm weight,
and the rise of our feathered hearts.

Tell Me

There are many people who spend their nights
on the subway trains. Often one encounters
them on the morning commute, settled in corners,
coats over their heads, ragged possessions heaped
around themselves, trying to remain in their own night.

This man was already up, bracing himself against
the motion of the train as he folded his blanket
the way my mother taught me, and donned his antique blazer,
his elderly, sleep-soft eyes checking for the total effect.

Whoever you are—tell me what unforgiving series
of moments has added up to this one: a man
making himself presentable to the world in front
of the world, as if life has revealed to him the secret
that all our secrets from one another are imaginary.

A Pole, a Fence, a Bridge

The man on the small tractor in the rose
garden recommends that I take a shortcut
through the woods. He shuts off the motor
and considers, then tells me I want to head
back up the hill to where I see the leaning pole.
Across from the pole is a footpath that will lead
me past a wire fence enclosing an off-limits
yard full of equipment; this will make it seem
that I'm going somewhere I'm not supposed to go.
But I want to stay on the path, which will bend
at the last moment away from the daunting fence
to reveal a high stone bridge over the river.
I want to cross the bridge, cut through the woods,
and bingo—there I am back where I started.

What is unusual about these instructions
is the fact that I am receiving them
inside New York City limits. Directions
in the city involve numbered names of streets
accompanied by a litany of *rights*
and *lefts*. Navigating by landmark
is a country method—objects that appear
one by one like a soothsayer's dream: the abandoned
white house, the newfangled blue silo, the lone tree,
the roadside cross, the empty rowboat anchored
in the middle of the pond. But here, too, in the Bronx
Botanic Garden, which, the brochure tells us, occupies
250 acres, it is possible to divine
direction with stories dropped like seeds.

Body Elite

For years I belonged to a neighborhood gym
in Brooklyn: a brownstone transformed, crooked floors
and all, by weight machines, rubber matting,
turquoise paint galore, a youthful staff eating
take-out from the Italian place next door.
I'd thread my way between body builders
taut and ornery as prize boars, performing
my 20-pound reps, invisible, as I assumed.

When I moved to Manhattan I dropped the gym,
but emerging from the subway one evening
I glimpsed a man I recognized, a silent
lifter of light weights who never socialized—
compact of body and purpose—whose face
in the crowd shone back like a private moon.

The Hungarian Pastry Shop & Café

is the only place I know in the city
where you can still see people with pen
and paper. Legal pads, spiral bound,
plain or college-ruled loose leaf, well-thumbed sheaves
of paper at every crumb-strewn table: précis,
postulations, undergraduate observations, sound
doctoral theory, a shady spot of fiction—
each hand the only one in the world
to produce such symbols, personal as finger-
prints, errant *y*'s and flighty *t*'s,
g's trailing their tails like apprehensive
dogs. It's a deep, low-ceilinged room, illuminated
dimly by porcelain snowdrops on the walls,
a foreign spring, ripe with words' secret burning.

Everything but God

In Europe you can see cathedrals
from far away. As you drive toward them
across the country they are visible—stony
and roosted on the land—even before the towns
that surround them. In New York you come
upon them with no warning, turn a corner
and there one is: on 5th Avenue St. Patrick's,
spiny and white as a shell in a gift shop; dark
St. Agnes lost near a canal and some housing
projects in Brooklyn; or St. John the Divine,
listed in every guidebook yet seeming always
like a momentary vision on Amsterdam
Avenue, with its ragged halo of trees, wide stone
steps ascending directly out of traffic.

Lately I have found myself unable
to pass by. The candles' anonymous
wishes waver and flame near the entrance, bright,
numerous, transitory and eternal
as a migration: the birds that fly away
are never exactly the same as those that return.
The gray, flowering arches' ribs rise
until they fade, like bones so large and old
they belong to an undetected time
on earth. Here and there people's small backs
in prayer, the windowed saints' robes' orchid
glow, the shadows—ghosts of a long nocturnal
snow from a sky below which we did not yet
exist, with our questions tender as burns.

Historic New York Pub Still Flourishing

The bright red picnic tables outside the White
Horse Tavern on Hudson Street are ready
for customers, their paint as glossy as if it were
not the end of the season—almost October—
with the sun, bright but no longer burning, falling
down over everything except where the blue
umbrellas cast their shade. A woman of sixty
or so, with a violet permanent bob and sunglasses,
a sturdy figure in a high-necked paisley dress,
hesitates on the sidewalk, checking and rechecking
a scrupulously clipped newspaper item, as if
the old neon horse's head over the door—unlit
at present, but unmistakable—is not sufficient
proof that this is the place she has traveled so far to reach.

Harvest

It must be a good year, somewhere,
for cherries. In a blue bowl on the table
they are turning from red to black
as the light goes, each stem tipped
with a minute fist clenching the air.
They keep coming—on every corner fruit cart
in New York City, every Korean
deli, all the bodegas and gourmet
stores—everyone has them to overflowing
this summer, these Grade A cherries that gleam
like newels and crack like cane, firm as beef
between your teeth. Impossible to know
who grew them, in what country down south where people
pick them by hand, one by one, too precious to taste.

How We Memorize

The woman sitting opposite me
on the subway is young enough
that lack of sleep can still pale and soften
her face like a child's. Her black violin
case rests upright on the floor between her legs,
looking like the most expensive thing
about her, with her corduroys balding
at the knees, the navy-surplus pea coat,
the stretched and pilling winter scarf.
A music score, encased in plastic, is open
on her lap. She glances down, her eyes taking
in one passage at a time, then closing—shell
pink eyelids trembling as though gently disturbed
by the outermost edge of an incoming tide.

On another day, an old actor sits
with his script in its three-ring black binder,
the highlighted lines plentiful enough
that he must have a decent supporting
role. His leather jacket dates back forty
years, at least, worn in freckles to the hide,
his Oxford scarf flung rakishly, leaving
his neck bare. He, too, looks down carefully
and then up, snapping his eyes shut, mouth
shaping silent sounds. The soft folds of his throat
ripple, as if words are pebbles and memory
water. One way or another, we mark
the things we love, like channels with buoys, trails
with blazes on trees, days with hours, bodies with stones.

Bicentennial

Who told me we'd be given free tricorn hats?
I don't remember, any more than I do
wanting one. But I must have, or I
would not have cadged my mother's ruffled white
pearl-buttoned blouse, badgered her to make
me a vest out of the red coverlet
off the day bed, completed my outfit with blue
flared corduroys and wool-lined winter boots.

It was going to be a battle—the dead
British to be played by kids from P.S. 8—
no—a parade—a march—a drill beside
the Brooklyn Bridge—a rumor, as it transpired,
marooning us, Minutemen *sans* hats, loose
change in the deepening pocket of the past.

Composed upon Brooklyn Bridge, July 6, 2003
(after Wordsworth)

How the city's infinite motions seem stilled
in the sun's horizontal blue gaze—her tips
and contraptions, her manifold upright lips'
lisp of steel and breath on sky, her curved sill
of shoreline, bridged and built as if the mills
of God have been replaced by quicker equipment,
her people heading home; now, before the dip
of the sun spills red, how this equal light wills
me to see the whole as one. For an instant,
her interlocking parts of bedrock and air,
asphalt and wind, metal and flesh, infant
cries of traffic and windows' crowded stare—
all these seem to pause and fuse, a jubilant
pair of mighty lungs with breath upheld in prayer.

Three

WIND FARM

Season's Greetings from South Dakota

To appear in my grandmother's Christmas
letters, you must be either giving
birth or newly dead; the act of living
doesn't pass the holiday litmus test

she keeps to the right of her typewriter
on the folded Singer sewing machine
by the window, where winter birds feed
as all in capitals she batters

data onto cold carbon-backed paper.
Why does it matter if she thinks of me—
a very smart rat in the city's maze
of intellects, subsisting on reading,
unnerved by silent Sundays in my cage—
while she invents extinction in the species?

Water Bug

Its carapace scratches the back of the bookcase
in my bedroom. I lie in the closed dark
listening for its ascent up the wall—
an old sound, significant of stealth—
small lives armed with segmented shells
surviving time to arrive unharmed in the vault
of now: broken cigarette smoke, Cutty Sark
melting in a glass, grown-ups' voices erasing

themselves in a distant room. Its jointed
shape will emerge, antennae first,
gelid red scarab in the gloom above my bed;
laughing mouth of a bug, yawn of dread
in its soft jaws, party to night's worst
dreams and the evolution of disappointment.

Inside

Through a lace curtain are a thousand cells
of blue, what is infinite parsed gravely
as an English lesson finished to save
time in science class—DNA of jelly

fish, bean-shaped mitochondrion. I can tell
myself after twenty-odd years
it's the powerhouse of the cell. Here
at my window, lace's shadows spilling

across my hands on the white table,
still are papers with words on them, sun
drowned, surrounding me, made-up
lessons. Out there, the sky's undone
every day, pouring itself away
in a lush absence of speculation.

Farmers ✓

That hits the spot conjures meat and potato meals
with my relatives—hale seniors plowing back
from the table, replete with protein
and starch—old-fashioned but accurate.
You might stretch the phrase to mean a cup
of black coffee on a cold day, or scenery
loved and left behind but grafted
to the tongue like taste; a correctly placed caress
or fall of rain. But if pressed, do you say
the spot exists? Or call it metaphor—the space
where need and happiness combine
somewhere between the belly and the mind,
describe it indirectly, use a corny phrase, to save
a seed of feeling—the small green spear of grace.

Wind Farm

Driving to my grandmother's funeral, we passed
a wind farm. It was dusk. The road ran straight
over the land, a smooth path between shorn blue fields
and fields still standing with bleached-out stalks of corn
waiting for the night combine with its headlights,
farmers taking the ears at their peak moisture
content—so delicate that even one more dew
will change it. My grandmother died in her sleep
unexpectedly and was found the next morning
when she missed bingo. From the back seat my mother
said, "Look," and the windmills appeared: one, two,
two hundred craning sleek and white out of the gloom,
wheeling with avian patience, as if all there was
was this task—to pull power from the sky and release it.

Tante Ethel in the Willow

She must have been as near seventy
as makes no difference to the child I was.
Her navy Keds dangled above our heads
for an instant. Then she was up behind
the green leaves' lace—two bare arms and a sleeveless
cotton blouse flouting the shivers of light.
She was always the tomboy recalled a sister
on the ground. Dead many years her husband,
Herm, had farmed with her—best-natured my father
said, of all his uncles. But he was just a name
to me, messenger of the gods on a tractor,
illustrated with winged boots. Around us bolts
of gold and blue plummeted from inestimable
heights, as angels throw down their hearts
                                    on the promise of more.

You Are Here

They say I could travel to Africa
on four hundred milligrams of quinine
a day—two pills methodically aligned
between my plate and my water glass—

isosceles triangle, mathematics
equation, white chalk drawn on green reminds
me that in the process of divining
hope we have to make a diagram, map

of my body, pale secret continent
unnavigated before pain began—
hot rain, dry frost, whichever way you went
there was a bone crack you could not cross, sand
so deep you could not walk, one message sent
back: *am alone now, cusp edge of God's hand.*

Beiderbecke, Leon Bismarck "Bix," 1903–1931

(b. Davenport, IA)

They find him on the floor, curled around his horn,
talking to it as if it were a drunken date
or a friend threatening suicide, pale
and unshaven. When they try to pick him up,
brush the New York studio dust off his clothes
(never spruce at the best of times), he pours
through their musicians' hands like water
or song. Improvisation is what matters
to him—finding the out, then walking back in the door
when least expected. But life on those terms
teaches too much about absence, how a tune's abrupt
close at three minutes can hide your failings
from everyone but you, how those 78s
spin into darkness grooved with the distance from home.

Needle and Thread

I am the accidental heiress
to my great aunts' dish towels and tea
cloths. So many tiny stitches—
how could one dry dishes, or do whatever

one does with tea cloths, on the back
of such artistry? The seven earnest cats
performing their household tasks, one for each day
of the week—how to touch water to that fine creweled

fur? Rumple those hand-embroidered whiskers? Would one
ever risk the linen squares trimmed with crocheted blue
and yellow lace beneath a pot of Darjeeling?
What to do with the trumpet-vine dresser scarf? I hate
to sew, myself—but if I don't use them, who will?
My only child is the ragged edge of time.

On Learning to Go Limp in Public Places

The details of the disease are the least
of it. It's this thirst for rest that teaches
lessons: how to measure energy
in a glass cup, how to forgo
impulse, to sculpt days precise as snow
fall on a park bench, in waiting
rooms, on buses and trains, in niches
of old buildings—to make little nights
out of daylight, sweet tea of half sleep—anywhere
flashing squares of windows suggest
the future, vast and burning *(who cares who's*
looking) with the rubied translucence of carousel
horses, turning only to return, insistent
tale bearers, alive as you or me.

Coming into Sioux Falls, South Dakota, in a Propeller Plane

At the time—1969—the idea
of the infinite didn't come into it.

Having changed from a jetliner
in Minneapolis to this smaller,
dimmer, louder plane, I felt only
immediate sensations: a buzz
in my body that increased when I touched
the wall with its constellations of gold
stars, the damp, smoke-filled air and its chill
on my legs, bare beneath the summer dress
I'd carefully chosen that morning in New York—
already a dream. Through a blinding blue window
hatched with fine silver threads the sky spread
in an even line over the yellow and green
squares of ground—like a picture in a book.

As the plane came down on uneven stairs
of air, I looked for the solitary roads and cars
and barns to which my attention had been drawn
to distract me from my stomach. The land was
so bare I could see the individual
weeds bent by the same wind that briefly lifted us

up as we hung over the runway, so real
as, roaring, our wheels touched the earth
and our propellers became visible, I can
still feel the lumbering U-turn we made
toward the terminal, not knowing I'd remember.

Van Gogh's Sunflowers

Whether it was a great aunt's sunflowers
copied from van Gogh and given pride
of place in the living room of her duplex
on North Freeman, or the paint-by-number
dogs left hanging in the pine-paneled
basement after my grandmother died,
I noted, as a child, only the fact
of their existence. Even as a young woman
I viewed them as stray clues to a trail gone cold:
the table lamp made from glass marbles baked
until they broke to shatter light like water.
Now, I do not doubt my ability to read truth
in fragments; the explanation of desire
renews itself, if you let it, like good blood.

Discovery

When the phone call comes I am on my knees
in the bathroom scrubbing the tub. The bath mat
is inadequate protection against
the tiles, as well as being damp. Damp blue
towel, hard blue floor, knees that feel sore
more quickly than they used to. Hoped for,
but not expected, the call represents
a miracle—never mind what kind—fill in
the blank: money, love, success—whatever
you've tried at 3 A.M. not to covet,
and failed. So here I am, bent like any soldier
to protect my vitals, accustomed to the daily
digging in—it's the surprise of change that makes
good fortune and bad luck feel the same.

The Distance

My mother read me poems before memory,
so maybe that's when it began,
the certainty that seemed already in
place at the time of my first memory—

or at least the two coincided exactly:
the earnest sound of her voice reading
fell like rain on the unmoving
earth of my conviction that poetry

was the highest object of humanity.
It was shocking, how she allowed spaces to fall
between the living words—spaces that started small
but lengthened to such silent immensity

that a poem became the distance
between what we must say and what we can.